Not Your Grandfather's

Guide to

Small Business Marketing

Not Your Grandfather's

Guide to

Small Business
Marketing

How to engage potential clients in a social media and
review-centric environment

Michel Gunn

I would like to dedicate this book to my mother and my husband, both of whom always see the silver lining in everything. My mother taught me to see it this way for others. I have carried this lesson with me into my work, where it has supported my efforts to consistently convince business owners to adopt a different point of view and present their offering in a way that will make them more profits.

Table of Contents

Why this book was necessary

I've picked up too many marketing books that talk about 'focus group budgets' and 'availability of databases,' from corporate marketing people that have no clue how a small business markets with lower budgets, to stay competitive.

I had to write a book to lend insight to small businesses to market better. I don't like the statistic that 69% of small businesses fail. I spoke once at a college where the professor's first conversation with me was about how most of the small business owners in the room would not amount to a successful business. We can't think like this, even though statistics are against us, especially not when corporate America gets so many of their bright ideas from these amazing start-ups. Time to give small businesses a realistic view on how to do better marketing to lower that percentage.

I meet too many business owners who have accepted the fact that they will never retire. If you feel this way, then this book isn't for you.

Being lazy or short sighted doesn't build legacies.

What you're going to learn in this book

Have you spent thousands of marketing dollars but aren't sure what you got from it? If so, you're going to learn strategy and tactics for marketing. Basically, I'm talking about the ideas behind results, and how to implement.

The reality is that business owners aren't marketing experts. The art and science of marketing is not something to be taken lightly. There are philosophies governed by behavioral and political environments that are seldom understood by owners or those involved too closely in the day-to-day business. Given this, it isn't a surprise that you are unhappy with your marketing efforts.

Here are 8 common mistakes made by owners doing their own marketing:

1. *You just open a flower shop business because you like flower arranging.*

   Just because you have a passion for something doesn't mean that people will see value in it (the way you do). You must make sure you have a business that offers value to the demands of the environment. You can use advertising to change people into thinking they need your product or service. But, if there is really no demand for it, you'll need to put a much larger amount of money into its marketing.

Solution: Conduct surveys, focus groups, give away the product/service. Basically, any activity that will give insight into the recipient's thoughts, you need to start collecting.

2. *You decide you want a brochure because your competition has one.*

As a business, you are struggling to figure out what marketing materials to use, so you look towards a competitor. This is one of the biggest mistakes business owners make. They copy their competition. If the competition is bigger and more established, and you have the same marketing materials, why would customers come to you? Your target customers will go to the bigger business. Later we talk about ways of doing something different to stand out.

3. *You consider 'Networking Group Dues' as your 'Marketing Campaign'.*

We live in an environment where social media is a strong force in advertising. This has increased the amount of time it takes to influence a person into buying. In other words, diversity should be in your advertising efforts. Networking can be one, but not your *only* marketing effort, to truly grow your business. Here are some platforms to market your business on and a few examples of how to do so.

A. Facebook posting - TIPS

B. LinkedIn posting - TIPS

C. Retargeting on FB Advertising

D. Messenger on FB

E. Website

F. Website blog writing

G. Review Aggregate Sites: (when you search for your business keywords, see what comes up like **Yelp**, Angie's list, ALA, American Lawyer Assoc., American Architects Association, Houzz.com)

H. Google Maps

I. Local SEO

J. SEO programs

K. Remarketing Google Advertising

L. Brochures/ Leave Behind pieces

M. Editorial pieces in local magazines

N. Advertising in community Magazines

O. Advertising in specialized magazines

P. Billboards in targeted areas

Q. Charity opportunities

R. Direct Mailers

S. PR... Any story can be made, such as "We just bought a cabinet in the new office that is in line with our business mission of creating great environments that develop helpful pleasant phone operators and designers."

T. Posters at the Sports club, if this is where your targets hangout.

U. Event tables. Tie in the event theme and then have other information on other offerings with you. Hire people to work with you.

V. Cooperative advertising with resources complementing your offerings

W. Campaigns to make connections – physical lunches, a candy bowl you fill weekly at your supplier's office, so they don't forget you, etc.

4. *Small businesses don't research enough*

The web is a wealth of information. Research other owner's experiences. Ask questions like 'what do people think of flower arranging?" You'll get a list of the `10 top tips from a national leader in flower arranging. Extrapolate what they have done that worked.

Find the "most profitable flower arranging business model" from companies like entrepreneur.com and other small business foundations that publish 'how to' articles. Also find high traffic areas for selling flowers, as well as the best fresh flower suppliers that you can learn from.

Finding mentors from whom to learn, is also important. What marketing worked for them, and why?

5. *Campaigns aren't thought through.*

Example: You suggest to the owner of the business to showcase flowers in churches to get exposure. The owner likes the idea, although you didn't research to find out that on any given Sunday, there are only 6 people in the congregation.

Every aspect needs to be researched. Taking the time to do this will save you money and get you more return on your investment.

6. *Forgetting that increases in sales and revenues, and not branding or logos, are the goals of marketing.*

Take the time to evaluate marketing programs and make sure there is a positive return on investment. Branding, like a new logo, isn't making sales.

One area that small businesses tend to get wrong is in thinking that branding and logos equals marketing. This keeps them stuck in trying to outdo their competitor's branding, because they think this is what will make a difference. If they see their competitor's sign is a little crooked, they'll think, "oh, my neighbor's sign is down. Now all I need to do is put up a sign that looks better, do a little branding, and that will get more customers into my store". But that will never happen. Business people who think like this, are hobbyists, and they will never retire because they are just breaking even, if at all.

Don't get trapped in this type of thinking. Decide what your goals are and how hard you are willing to work to change your business from a hobby to a business. I meet too many business owners that are happy doing their marketing by themselves and have accepted the fact that they will never retire. This book isn't for them.

You do not need to struggle with doing your marketing.

It is hard to work on sustainable growth of your business while trying to run it. That is why you should go for intelligent marketing. That is, focus on managing the business and bring in a marketing agency for your marketing.

The environment changes constantly. The 'Not Your Grandfather's Guide to Small Business Marketing' is thus named because your grandfather, who might have started the business, was operating on a set of rules for his time. We know that the attention span of people today is 2 to 3 seconds, during which time you need to get them your message. Your grandfather's marketing tactics are outdated and cannot compete with such dynamics. You'll see however, their fundamentals are still within the strategies I speak of.

Although, as we speak, this book is starting to get old. So, let's get to it and help your business.

.

Chapter 1

Why your marketing isn't working.

Issue: Your marketing isn't working as well as you want. Have you spent thousands of dollars and are not sure what you got from it?

Solution: Look at everything. Be your worst critic.

Impact on Your Business: You will grow.

The biggest Issue we see from marketing agencies that suck you in and take a lot of your money with little to show for it, is that they are trying to please YOU, the owner or marketing director of your small business. They cozy up to your ego and fill it.

So, they 'pump you up' with things like a great brand video, and a website that says great things about you, and you get very excited. In reality, *you are marketing to yourself, and not selling anything that your customer wants.* This is not going to grow your business.

You must stop and think. Ask yourself what you have given to the customer or shown to the 'potential' customer. All you have done, is you have shown them how great you are and now you think they will buy into you, because you're great.

Well, it doesn't work that way. It is nice that you like seeing yourself on your brochure. But, what good does that do for your customer? It's time to *understand that real marketing talks about the needs and feelings of your customer, not you.*

So how do you apply this and shift your thinking to make a great video, or an amazing website which now engages and invites customers for a lifetime of positive reactions about you *and* your brand?

Here is a checklist to start your analysis:

1. Identify who your customer is.

   a. Are they male? Female? Have Children? Married or single?

2. How would they use your product?

3. How would your product make their lives more fulfilled and happy?

4. When you market does it increase your sales?

5. Do your customers become lifetime customers procured through advertising?

6. Are you making sure you are pleasing the customers?

7. Are you listening to what they want?

When you don't like the answers to these questions, work on solutions to change that. Learn what marketing really means to your customers. Give them what they want from you. In chapter 5, we'll talk about 'being their guide', which is a great way to deliver your information.

Someone that is an example of this:

A fire equipment provider decides they want to generate business through a website. They keep getting calls from Google Adwords agents selling them $99/m of Adwords. How this Adwords advertising works is that they give you the same words as other businesses in your niche. Then, when it doesn't work, they tell you that you're not spending enough and that you need to increase the budget... On a bad marketing ad campaign. So, the fire equipment company was given the same words as other fire equipment businesses, and the agents didn't even ask what made them different. This didn't go well at all; they didn't get the customers they wanted yet they were spending money. But they only found this out 3 years later and thousands thrown away.

These one-off agents that sell you 'one-action' programs like Adwords, are usually a money pit that never really works. So, stop doing it and put the money somewhere else that will work, or bring in a proven Google Adwords agent.

If your marketing isn't working, make changes. Review your initiatives every month if you can't do it weekly.

Chapter 2

Why your phone operator is the wrong person to be making marketing decisions.

The *right* people, with the *right* education and *the right* skills, are crucial to successfully marketing your business.

Issue: You want to include 'the staff' in marketing decisions because you heard it is healthy. The reality is that they stand between you and real business growth because their job security is threatened when qualified persons are hired to help.

Solution: Understand this as an owner. You must make hard decisions sometimes, to move forward. To reach real growth, hire a proprietary marketing-educated person or team to fully concentrate on your business marketing. Even if you train your staff, they should only complement the expertise you are getting from qualified marketing agencies.

Impact on Your Business: Business grows faster and healthier if staff members in defined positions have clear responsibilities on how to work as a marketing team.

So many owners of small businesses rely on their phone attendants or project managers to weigh in on their marketing initiatives.

There is a huge risk in doing this. Your staff are probably making just over minimum wage, or somewhere in the average zone of pay, and…. Now you want them to think about building your company, say to $8 million/yr. Do you see the Issue?

At minimum wage, you could be asking too much of them to grow your business. Besides, staff members become complacent with time and will rarely go over and beyond what's contained in their job description. If their job says print brochures, that's what they'll do; they will not think about how they need to be doing more to make an $8 million-dollar goal.

So, if you expect them to grow your business, you might be failing yourself because it is very likely all they want to do is make their minimum wage and go home. Their interests might not be aligned with yours.

Needless to say, if you have identified someone in your company who has the capacity to help build your business, send them for marketing classes. –Although for substantial growth, you'll need marketers with experience and proven track records.

By hiring a marketing expert, you are trying to avoid being reactionary. A marketing expert deals with the long-term view of things. They see beyond the daily tracking and analysis. Their focus, is in creating strategies that support you to pursue your mission statement. But if you're dealing with your phone operator, their focus is on the here and now. If you had rolled out some serious marketing campaigns the previous week, they may be long forgotten the moment your phone operator gets new issues raised on the phone.

A marketing expert will handle this by having the person bring the topic to a strategy meeting.

Even your other staff members might not be suitable to work at strategy level. For instance, marketing agents spend all their time on training and devising ways to push your product/service, so you can expect them to keep their eyes on growth goals. The administrative manager can provide information to marketing campaigns lending a customer's points-of-view. They are a source of insider knowledge that can help the marketing team leader, but that is all they can be.

Putting someone on the job as marketing, while they are also the one managing daily project activity, does not allow them time and background to fully think outside the box. If anything, they are too inside the box, and are influenced by what closely affects their primary job.

So, although you think you don't have the budget, until you get serious and employ or hire a marketing agency to partner with, and to train your staff on growth strategies, you will struggle with reaching your goals.

Someone that is an example of this.

We consulted on a marketing project once, for a local $4.2M wood and metal care maintenance company. They were 35 years old and looking to reach the next level of business growth. Our task was to formulate an aggressive growth marketing plan and some element creation.

But they had an Issue. –They were relying on family members and tenured employees with years of service, none of whom had marketing experience.

For a move of this magnitude, there was a need for real expertise in the field of marketing. The right way to handle this was to have an external marketing agency come in and as part of their package, train the tenured employees, who could then assist in implementing parts of the initiatives.

Initially, meetings were set up with the owners and the 'marketing person' who was one of the staff members. This marketing person also happened to be the same one charged with answering the phones (the phone operator). They were also the same person who had to order brochures and set up a photographer to get images of their work.

The operator felt threatened. –This is a common reaction when you use members of staff such as your phone operator, to be your marketing contact. They hear all these marketing ideas, but they don't have a say in the major decisions. This in turn, can lead to confrontation and prevent proper implementation of initiatives.

In this case, the owner was not able to handle the push back and instead put on hold the opportunity for substantial growth, so as not to upset anyone.

This is also another trait that is very common with owners of small businesses. They don't want to upset the ones doing the day-to-day work and they settle for substandard moves until they have too many years of stagnation or loss of growth.

To break down this opposition, have the marketing agency build in training so that staff members become a part of the work.

Marketing, as you are learning in this book, involves human behavior principles. Your employees, who have helped you build your business to agreeable numbers, will most likely be able to add onto, but never run very effective campaigns.

Realize that everyone has their part to play. If you are a flooring service provider, just as you wouldn't depend on a marketing business to shine your hotel lobby wooden floors, is the same way you wouldn't hire your floor polishers to market for you.

Since taking the decision to suspend marketing plans, the wood and metal maintenance business is still in stagnation.

Chapter 3

Your sales goals must come first in all marketing decisions.

Issue: Your goal is defined only by the word 'growth'. We want to grow, but we haven't put numbers on paper.

Solution: Set quantifiable goals and start planning initiatives that will help to achieve them.

Impact on Your Business: You will have clarity that will influence your business offerings, focus the business, meet goals, and establish a sustainable real identity.

First set goals. Then analyze the business, and the offerings to determine the value of the customers plus what it takes to maintain them. These calculations are the variables used to set out what is required to reach the goals.

So, start answering these questions:

1. What are your Goals - How big do you want to be?

- Volume $ figure you'd like your business to be within the 1st year?

- 3 years?

- 5 years?

2. How much growth can you handle in a short period of time?

3. Who are your customers? Create a pool of targets to which you'll assign a value. When they have a value, you can then plug it into an equation to figure out how each pool will help you to reach your growth number.

- Take Starbucks for example. Their customers are people that like strong coffee while enjoying an inspiring atmosphere to do everything from meeting others, to working. So, on a daily basis a Starbucks customer is worth $10 on average (coffee and drink). They visit 3 times a week. $30 a week multiplied by 52 weeks is $1560. They know their traffic is 200 people a day. That is 1400 visits a week at $1560 a person equals $2,184,000 annual revenue per store. So, if they want incremental growth, _ say $200,000 more in a given year _, they can plan to upsell to current clients and or introduce a new drink to attract a new target group.

Now go back to *your* goals and do the math. How do I make $2,000,000 this year targeting my clients that we value at \_$X_?

Customers can also be valued based on their lifetime of patronizing your business. Do your numbers and your campaigns will be goal oriented. You must also get serious about analyzing these goals so that if your results are good, you can continue with the campaigns and if not, you can move on to better marketing initiatives.

Example of a firm that experienced this:

A Dental firm of 4 dentists approached our marketing company. They wanted to open a new office that would cost them around $2Million to build.

We asked them to start doing their numbers. They had a few strategies that came to the surface once we started with questions based on client value. They knew if they specialized in crowns they'd make $5,000 per client on average. So, they targeted a demographic of adults around the ages of 40 to 60 years of age. They also knew that new customers with the more expensive 'Blue Empire' insurance had many more benefits including some cosmetic procedures, so targeting these clients by working with the insurance company would lead to upsells and again a better value to them.

So, just with a few values pegged to certain clients, they were able to start focused campaigns resulting in growth that was well planned.

They achieved growth and were able to fund the new office in a year's time.

Chapter 4

Be your own dog. The worst marketing strategies are the ones exactly like your competitor's.

A fresh canvas is inspiring. Don't let competitors influence you.

Issue: I'm not as established as my competitor, so I don't have the resources, marketing, or understanding to step 'outside of what I see them doing'. I'm scared to take a risk and do something different, although my business is not growing despite my efforts.

Solution: Do something different that will make you stand out and help you establish your business as special. Read case studies to help you get confident about moves.

Impact on Your Business: You will build REAL strategies that build a brand.

There is a 'best practices' concept that influences your business and shouldn't be

21

ignored. Customers will check up on you online and if you don't have certain automatic credible appearances, you could be hurting your business. Best practices in marketing applies to every business. For instance, as an electrician, you should be on the county's certified electrician online listing of accredited contractors. If you are a gym, you should invest some money in the local athletic magazine directory. You could also send the November postcards to capture the 'Jan work-out goal' trend that happens every year like clockwork.

I'm just saying that not all strategies should be going against the grain to stand out. There are some obvious places that any business could market itself and these can give you a lot of visibility. But, if some of these obvious places don't work, don't invest in them even though other businesses seem focused there. For example, if the local newspaper is not working for you, don't invest in it.

Now let's talk about what 'being your own dog' entails. It means stepping out of your comfort zone. Be the new gym that give seminars at schools, about how to run a trending obstacle race. Let the kids take home the handsome brochure that includes a cool coupon to buy a 'fitbit'. While doing all these new things, your targets, and your mission, should be top of mind. If you want to target more families to join your gym, you could offer child athletic training for

Varsity sports athletes and include an offer to the parents for a reduced 3 months to try the gym.

With ALL services, even products, there is a habit-forming element that you have to tap into. Gym memberships are very habit driven; although, so is getting an electrician, accountant and lawyer. Create something exciting that is different than what your competitor is doing.

So, back to the 'don't follow your competitor's marketing'... The competitor might be fully established in their market share. Think of it like trying to win over a girl. You're the 'other guy'. You won't offer the girl the same thing as the guy you are trying to outcompete. You'd offer something that will really make her choose you. What is that thing in your business?

Whether you are stealing market share from a dinosaur that still thinks that the whole world wants them, or you are the guy that is offering something new, be exciting. Do your homework and understand what would really make your potential customers excited about using you... and be different.

Example of someone that experienced this:

A landscaper of ours decides he wants to expand his business to Chappaqua, NY. Well, there is an established landscaper there that has been servicing the area for 35 years. First the new landscaper decides to study this competitor's style and imitate it in his advertising. He gets no business. Why? because he is offering exactly what the established guy is.

So, the battle begins between old landscaper guy with his own style and tons of proven successful happy clients, and the new guy with no history of this type of landscaping in the area, so he doesn't have a value that people could pursue.

The new guy comes to our marketing agency and we show him how if he starts offering different exciting varieties of plants, and a One-Day no-hassle installation, this would be a reason to make people consider him over his competitors. You always need a niche or specialty plus a WOW factor (we talk about in chapter 6) to set you apart. Tom's wow factor, was the new plants and easy installation that had the neighbors suddenly talking

To summarize, if you want to be your own dog, think like you're winning over a relationship pursuit. Consulting a marketing agency will spark ideas of which you hadn't considered.

Chapter 5

Be the expert. GUIDE your customers through the buying JOURNEY — don't boast.

Issue: I am showing all our business accomplishments. This worked to bring people in years ago, but it isn't working anymore for us. Again, your grandfather's ideas need an updating.

Solution: When you go on a first date, do you spend your evening boasting about your accomplishments? My guess is No. If you boast, they won't go on a second date with you. The same is the case with your customers. As much as they want to know about you, they don't want you to boast; they want to feel as though you are 'all about them'. If you want to nurture your 'relationship' with your customers, Play the role of the expert, and guide them through their journey. If you want them to Purchase your service/product, you must start by painting the picture of why you are the right person to solve a problem they are grappling with. So, start with defining the problem, then guide them to where you provide the final solution to it.

Impact on Your Business: Business growth that is sustainable because you started with understanding how your customer arrives at purchasing from you.

Learn from the millennials; embrace social media. Go online and Google your service or product and see the great amount of information that's out there on it. Because of the ease to acquire information and the social-ness of today's human interaction, marketing, more than ever, has taken a 'relationship building' format. There is no better way to nurture this relationship than with social media. Millennials understand this better than anyone; Social media is at the very essence of engagement with customers and buyers. This is definitely an avenue that should be use to guide them their 'journey' of finally purchase.

But, for all its connectedness, social media has made the cycle of selling a client longer than ever because there are options at their fingertips, along with information on your service. So how do you make it easier on yourself?

First, by understanding your potential new client's needs and orchestrating the process to final purchase. It is how customers will come to choose you over your competition.

Second, by being the guide. This allows the customer to still be in charge of their decisions. Guide them to that expert electrical service or to that surgical weight loss procedure. It is the only way that customers will have confidence in you. It is the only way you get to keep them in control of solving their problem, which puts them in the position of authority. The second you start boasting about your business, especially before customers haven't completely decided if you are their choice, you strip the empowerment of making a decision, and lose the sale. When they are interested in seeing who created the product or service that will solve their problem, then, is the time to boast and introduce your business' accomplishments.

Being the guide builds a 'relationship' and will secure longevity of your customers' patronage to your sales people and the business. The guidance should be in all the forms of marketing you are using. From the way you phrase your website to the script the salespeople use to close the deal.

So be the guide in this journey, and there are tons of practical ways you can do this:

For example, if you provide an electrical service, in your marketing, add tips on how to find the best electrician and why. This empowers the people at the beginning of the journey where they are just starting to look for help. They will remember it came from you.

If you are a renovation contractor, broadcasting the 15 steps it takes to make a vaulted ceiling with sound dampening shaping, will do multiple things. For one, it will portray you as the 'expert' your clients are seeking, and secondly, it will create a level of trust gained by 'trying to help out' your potential customers.

We could come up with a hundred other scenarios from every industry, but the point is, giving information on the right ways to do your job is very powerful. It gives people the knowledge they need to make the right decisions when choosing someone to help them with their task, whether it's after they tried to do it themselves, or just the fact that they needed to hear that you knew what you were doing.

So, write those tips as guidance to your customers, as often as you can and layer them into your marketing campaigns. Remember, hiring a marketing agency to write them will keep your target's interests at the forefront of topics.

Chapter 6

Find your 'WOW' factor. Get out of your comfort zone. You need to go to extremes to get people to fall in love with your product/service.

Issue: I can't keep customers

Solution: You need to find that *specific something* that makes your clients LOVE you.

Impact on Your Business: You build a culture that people really want and are proud to say they patronize.

It is not easy to change. Most small businesses are okay with 4%-5% incremental annual increases, although when you talk to them you realize how hard they are working just to keep this increase going. They are missing the WOW factor that builds sustainability. The wow factor should pop throughout the buyer's journey, especially toward the end.

Convincing them that you are right for them, is what you've work toward up to now. Pulling them over the edge is really all about giving them the feeling of a 'great deal' or 'opportunity'. –the WOW. There are many ways in which you can add WOW to your offerings.

For example, you could offer your current listings for free or at a minimal cost. Think again about Starbucks. They are a culture of strong coffee drinkers who like to sit and work. Some of the WOW factors that got them to the billion-dollar institution they are today, were: the first to give WIFI away for free, free refills within the same day, great music to work to, an ordering app to help you avoid lines, ... the smart marketing WOW-creation continues because they are very clear on what their goals and target customers.

This model could apply to any business. Say you are an electrician, you could give away $9.99/m service contracts -plus 2 free audits on the home. This not only makes your client feel protected by feeling as if they have a constant electrician, but it also gets your technician back in the home to upsell a service. This is sustainability of a business through WOW factors.

Example of someone that experienced this:

A landscaper invested in better fertilizer for the seasonal urns he designed and installed 4 times a year. The urns gushed with flowers, succulents, and other foliage. This WOW factor impressed not only the owners of the home, but the visitors, the other craftsman doing work on the home, and the neighbors. Pretty soon, they were telling others about him. Look at the reach of potential sales people, talking about you, just because you have found your WOW factor.

This is such an important aspect to getting ahead in your business.

I want to share another WOW-factor success story:

A personal injury law firm allocated budget for providing expert medical testimony from well-known doctors, even for cases with the lowest projected earnings. For the level of cases they were trying this was not the standard. This approach paid off; they won cases and made far beyond the $1500 they had conservatively estimated. This is their WOW factor that sets them apart from competitors. It is an upfront cost for the firm, but the results cover the cost 10 times over.

Chapter 7

Integrating different medias for marketing campaigns is key.

Issue: We mailed out a promotion to 10,000 people and got very little results

Solution: Campaigns need to be planned as a 'system' not just a direct mailer on its own. A campaign must be built around multiple medias.

Impact on Your Business: The culture of your business is built while *impacting*, not just selling your customer.

What is a marketing system? Here's an example of what it could look like:

1. Frequent 'tip' blog posts

2. Facebook advertisement giving a checklist to add to the tips, in which you collect an email to continue the conversation, again guiding them through the buying journey.

3. A testimonial broadcast of how someone else just like them, loved you because you follow through from your tips.

4. A 'history of the company' advertisement.

5. A price discount that is an exclusive 2-week only offer.

6. A follow up to make sure they did a great job with the product or service, with a tip on how to get on a preferred list to jump the line in the future for the same services.

These are various examples you might use. See how this has a 'relationship' type chain link system?

Now, the marketing elements with which to deliver them is dictated by the end recipient. It could be Facebook advertisements, Google and FB retargeted reminders (boots or fishing pool that chases you around the internet until you buy), a tip blog with a promotion at the end, a direct mail promotion to opt in for a coupon, a strong website with testimonials and reviews that convey it as a reliable business source. The point is, cover your story, by creating a full supported system, driving to one main result– Revenue.

How do you set up multiple elements?

Again, start with a PLAN.

Look at past marketing attempts. Use your goals. Take this information to the marketing team to plot out a plan for creating campaigns with marketing 'system' multiple elements.

Let's use the example of an electrician targeting home owners with generator installation:

Your marketing system could look like this:

1. Become a manufacturer's certified dealer and maximize this exposure.

    a. Use their marketing to get reviews
    b. Keep your profile updated with current jobs and description.
    c. Allocate more budget to the marketing campaigns that are working.

2. Mention upsells on customer invoices

    a. On your invoices, you should place an exclusive one-time promotion for generator servicing, in which customers could order immediately at a discounted rate.
    b. If they don't take you up on the offer immediately after the installation, then put their information into your system and target them with other forms of marketing, like email marketing and direct mail with the aim to close other sales later.

3. Make alliances with plumbers that are installing gas lines for kitchen renovations. Also, with contractors working on new kitchen and additions renovations. Generators need gas hook ups. What a great time to put in a second line to protect your new home improvement with a generator, which you're renovating.

4. Do FREE servicing of the businesses that will promote you. If your targets are home owners, think of their environments or hobbies that would identify with things they enjoy. Many home owners have dogs; hence they deal with SPCA. Go to the SPCA and donate your services in exchange for a spot in their marketing materials.

5. Blog tips on 'How to pick an electrician for your generator installation' or 'Recommended care for your generator', etc.

6. Advertise on Facebook, choosing demographics such as homeowner, age range and area of servicing. Then use the all-mighty intel and target their interest. Facebook is great at recording customers' interest and shopping behaviors. They are also great at providing you this information.

7. Set up a retargeting/remarketing campaign. It is inexpensive and highly effective in today's digital world. This is the fishing pole or pair

of boots that chases you around the internet because you showed interest in buying them.

8. Friend recommended

    a. Get reviews from clients. Get video reviews so you can post on video spots for more exposure.
    b. Incentivize. Ask clients to mention you on FB and other social media avenues, or share your page, in exchange for a discount or a reward. New clients who buy from you from the shared link should also receive a reward.

    Note: some social platforms have strict guidelines about paying for endorsements; be sure to follow the guidelines for endorsements and contests.

9. Architects and Contractors doing renovations can also be a source of recommendations. You can partner with them through creative methods such as:

    a. Set up lunch meetings to meet them.
    b. Have a program where they can earn something on the jobs which they refer to you.
    c. Include them in your marketing.

      d. Partner with them in *their* marketing. Pay them to put you in their marketing.

10. The Generator Company has a list of 'recommended contractors for installations'. Get yourself on that list and on any other marketing material you could add to your leave-behinds. As humans, we have a need to give to those we feel we owe. So, do for others, as it will come back to you in multiples.

11. Direct-to-Consumer selling of generators:

      a. Direct mailing right before a storm.

      b. Facebook advertising talking about the almanac's prediction of the cold winter and other premium pressure points of the targets. Addressing their fears of not having a generator, is one tactic you could use.

      c. When the weather starts turning colder, run Generator adverts on TV and Radio, talking about how keeping your family warm and secure will provide you a longer life and better relationship with your spouse.

Again, use multiple marketing medias to get different readings. Throw out the marketing elements that don't work.

Don't stop until you reach your goal.   Find different ways to steer the customer to the fact that you are the best business to install a customer's generator.

Example of someone for which a marketing 'system' worked:

The same landscaper we discussed in the previous chapter ran a Facebook Advertisement on a tip for mixing your own 'Organic Tick potion'.

This advertisement redirected to the blog on the landscaper's site, explaining the formula.   Then the blog offered 2 gallons of tick potion that they delivered and spread for you when you hired them for a $2000 landscaping design project.   It was a $100 value.

Because the first advertising of this campaign was successful, they also pushed out 5 videos on YouTube that were Search Engine Optimized (SEO'd).   These videos talked about ways to prevent ticks, along with some realities and understandings of why our region has gotten worse when it comes to tick colonies.   Still more positive results.

To add on to the successful campaign, direct mailers and commercials were made about the tick potion.

After applications were made, a post-campaign initiative of review retrieval was done.

The results showed that this use of multiple medias to push what was tested as a success in the beginning, exposed the same campaign reinforcing each element exponentially. In other words, the landscaper became *the* authority on organic tick potion, which was his way to bring in new customers, who would later make use of his full services.

Let's go back and list all the medias that were part of this exposure, which cemented this landscaper as the main distributor of this popular product, while formulating many leads for upselling their design and year-round services.

Media's used:

1. Blog-writing to get readership

2. Facebook Advertising

3. You-Tube Video

4. Lead-Page for information on product

5. Direct Mailer

6. Post-delivery Reviews of product and Landscaper

The results were a lead a day during a 2-month period. It was a highly successful campaign that also produced 10 new clients valued at $50,000 each.

Chapter 8

Why are CRM and MAS systems great for businesses of all sizes?

Issue: Your 'client tracking' system consists of whiteboards and sticky notes everywhere, which are too confusing. We need to review it daily to keep it organized. We aren't working on the actual work, but more on the system of what needs done.

Solution: Pick a Customer Relationship Management system, (CRM), or a Marketing Automation Software (MAS)

Impact on Your Business: Organize your business so that you can see what is and isn't working.

B asically, here is how investing in CRM and MAS can turn around your business:

CRM - Customer Relationship Management system. These range from expensive systems such as Salesforce and Hubspot CRM systems to those running off "off-off-Broadway" software like ZOHO.

Marketing Automation Software is a system to push customers through the sales funnel on a few digital pages. Click Funnels and Lead Pages are two systems that I like, currently.

CRM and MAS systems are great for providing
DATA
— and data, is POWER.

These systems help you map out marketing campaigns to target your potential customers through their buying journey for your product or service.

The top of the management system has profiles of people that might need your product or service but don't know it yet. You can use the system to reach and educate them on your offerings.

Then, using tracking and reporting tools build into the systems, you can monitor how customers respond to your efforts. You can even customize settings, so that you get more specific information from each response.

For example, you could add a link on an email or direct mailer, where customers can download a file by clicking on it. Your CRM/MAS system will log in all action related to the link and will target customers with relevant information and offerings to bring them closer to buying. For instance, when a customer clicks on the link, your CRM/MAS might offer them a coupon for your service or product.

So, in a nutshell, CRM/MAS are systems that you can use to reach potential clients through marketing automation, along with managing current in-house client accounts. In-house automations can be 'appointment reminders', or invoice processing, among others.

Though CRM and MAS were developed for big corporations, the small business community is the fastest growing sector for these systems. The demand for automation by smaller companies has prompted a generation of smaller versions, which are compact versions of their large predecessors.

Knowing and being able to react to the way that potential customers perceive your sales efforts, advertising and servicing—is priceless.

So, start asking around to find a 'Client Relationship Management' system. You'll thank me.

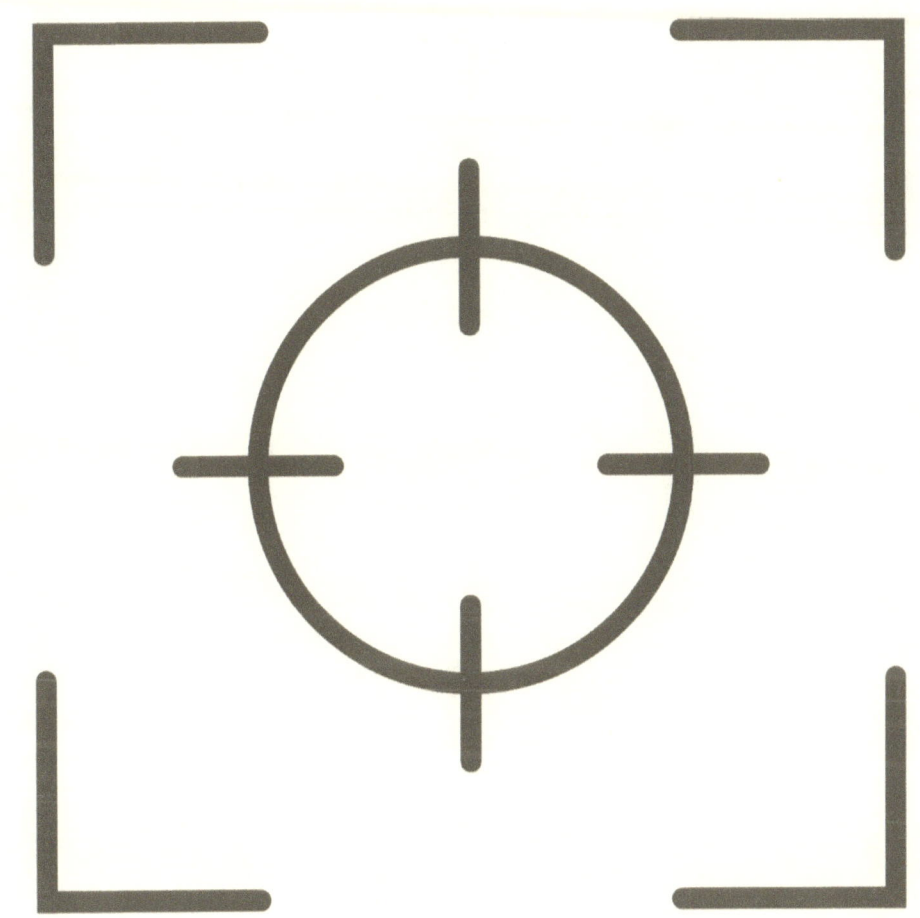

FOCUS

Chapter 9

How to gauge -the 'RIGHT' avenues to pursue the 'RIGHT' client

Issue: You think all people are good clients. You don't understand that certain people display characteristics positioning them as closer to buying than ones you will never land.

Solution: Define your customers based on a few criteria which puts them into these categories of 'lead temperature: cold, warm and hot.

Impact on Your Business: Focusing your marketing strategies which pursue clients more accurately and according to real needs. This increases the amount of sales you will close.

Here's how to start defining your potential customers.

Firstly, we need to define where your business operates at its most optimal; I call it your business' 'Sweet Spot'. This 'Sweet Spot' is found at the intersection of the following:

1. Least amount of output of labor to finish a job

2. Most profit from a job

3. Wow factor built into the job, to keep them coming back

Okay, so when you understand where your business' 'Sweet Spot' lies at your most efficient and profitable of services or products, connect it to whichever customers would most profit from this situation.

For example: The ABC College is best in agricultural engineering. This is the foundation on which ABC College was established. How that program works with little management is very profitable for them, because it is second nature at this point. So, a HOT lead as a client (student) connection to this engineering agriculture program, would be someone interested in botany and engineering. A WARM lead would maybe be someone wanting to 'manage' a business in Agricultural Engineering.

See how the management interest in slightly removed as it requires business management curriculum. It isn't an exact match to your offering, so you must sell your offering harder, making it a WARM versus a HOT lead.

And a COLD lead in this instance is someone who has no interest in any of these subjects, So ABC College should not waste time trying to sell them.

Lead Categories and another way to explain the differences in the category, in addition to how to handle them:

- **Hot Lead**

    - o *Definition:* someone who has answered a promotional ad and is ready to purchase.

    - o *Action to take:* Close these people first. Make the process to buy EASY.

    - o ***Example of marketing effort to push to hot:*** Immediately have dates available for your business to service them, while replying to their questions.

- **Warm lead**

    - o *Definition:* Someone who has done your quiz or answered a blog post. They have interest and are at the beginning of researching about your service/product.

    - o *Action to take:* Work on these people. Learn their interests and become an information source answering their demand. This will bring them closer to buying.

- *Example of marketing effort to push to Warm:* Put them into your marketing system, starting with the email marketing program.

- **Cold lead**

  - *Definition:* Someone who has shown no behavioral pattern of ever wanting or needing your service/product.

  - *Action to take:* No reason to try to get them interested. It will take too much labor and they may still not convert to a customer

  - *Example of marketing effort to push to Warm:* Open a different division offering them what they are looking for.

Now that you understand the difference in your potential clients, use their interest to build your campaigns.

Chapter 10

How to test marketing elements so you 'don't lose your shirt'

How to Test with 'the SMALL business' budgets.

Issue: You jump into a marketing campaign that the marketing agency made you believe could get you big results with limited budget or work.

Solution: You need to find a few lower-priced marketing elements that provide reporting to test different approaches to see what works best (A/B testing or split testing). Facebook advertising is one of these, currently.

Impact on Your Business: You will spread your budget wisely by scaling up on the best approach.

The testing process/cycle should flow as follows:

1. Test

2. Implement

3. Analyze the results

4. Adjust

5. Start again

Let's talk about the test.

Following this process will ensure you don't throw a lot of money at a marketing idea, just because someone has talked it up. Instead, approach the investment objectively; Have the person plan several marketing activities, split your money among these activities, and monitor which one has the best return-on-investment (ROI).

To be successful on Small business budgets, start small but invest in creating planned strategies. Think 'print direct mailers and targeted blogs with calls-to-action'. List exactly what you think a customer is looking for in your product. Remember that most people want something new looking—easy and fun to order—and that enhances their lives.

With that in mind, let's conduct an exercise that will help you give your customers what they want (conduct as much of this exercise on your own, but get your marketing agency to help as needed).

Build a profile of the target. Use your list of attributes of the target and devise text, images and a strategy to fulfill their need.

Create your direct mailer and blog. Go over it and make sure it is interesting (to them).

Tweak it. Have colleagues in marketing review and give an opinion. Tweak again.

Work on two versions to 'split test' and analyze which one works better. Put more funding into the one that works. Design others like this and test them.

As you work on the testing cycle, bear in mind the following:

Don't let up until you have succeeded in getting a good percentage of your target. 1% is almost a guarantee if you keep at it. 2% is a good return. 5% is great.

A great strategy for the test is to go to the people who've bought from you before and sell them a new service/product.

Another tactic is to go after a competitor's market share, and here, you can leverage your niche and WOW factor to stand out. Keep in mind that winning new customers is not the same as marketing to customers you already have. So, although you should maintain the same brand look and mission, build new profiles and create different marketing text, image and strategy from what has worked with existing customers.

Testing establishes real data which can be used to plan future marketing more accurately, to mean bigger goals, hence BIGGER WINS.

HAVE A PLAN

The 7-step Marketing Plan

People ask me how to start. Plan, plan, plan. You probably are sick of hearing me say this by now, but it is where every successful idea starts. This is also how this book fits together to achieve goals towards the next stage of your business.

Follow these steps and you will start thinking like a growing business.

Step 1

Before you get your employees and marketing team together, you should figure out the GOALS of your business and account for any threats. Your goals should include numbers that reflect realistic growth, while threats are any factors or services that you think will be detrimental to the bottom line.

Make sure all members of decision making capacity are gathered in this meeting.

Lay out all the marketing that you are doing currently. From Journal News, to Radio Ads, Facebook Ads, Brochures, direct mailer and others. Ask the marketing staff to put costs and measured results on post-its, for all the elements.

Rope in everyone in the company and let them know of plans and ways of working, going forward.

Step 2

Decide which marketing campaigns/elements aren't working and discontinue those.

Focus on the ones that are working and talk about how to go deeper into them and what it will take to make them succeed.

A comparative analysis between the campaigns that aren't working and those are working, will shed light on what you're doing right in the ones that are working.

Step 3

Work on making the growth areas easier to buy by the customer. Can they sign up and get immediate attention from the web? Can you eliminate long conversations by directing the customer to an intake form that auto-fills or that you can partially complete on their behalf?

How easily can you service their need? Can you now position the company to do same day response calls or visits?

Can you build an App or website chat to provide service 24/7 with answers and sign up options, so that you don't lose potential customers?

If you can answer yes to all these elements, this is an indication that the buyer journey is smooth. It's how you get MORE CONVERSIONS.

Step 4

Set up a system to change the 'maybe interested' customers to 'raving fans'. Make sure the plan has steps that address ways to keep the customer happy through the life of their journey with you and your company.

The system has these elements such as (yours may have more):

1. After they are directed to your website by an advertisement, monitor what pages they visit, to gain insight on their interest in a service/product.

2. Offer 'A lead magnet' such as a checklist on, "important things you can't do without." A list like this, strategically placed just before deciding to purchase a service/product, is very useful for collecting email. An email immediately goes out to them asking if they had a question on the service they were investigating.

3. This is followed by another email that offers a discount on that service.

4. They buy the service, which you have ensured is excellent and includes your WOW factor.

5. You ask them to fill out a 'Survey of our work' to understand what's working and how to improve on what's not working. And possibly if they are very happy, ask for a public review. People are happy to review when they know it will better serve their community in the future, so be sure to mention that when you ask for a review.

Insist that everything you do in marketing follows this process all the way through.

Step 5

Get the right people to do the right jobs. If employees or contractors aren't doing the job to turn results, start thinking about what you are looking for in a team or person that can change this.

Step 6

Hire a marketing agency to lay out goals, your mission statement and your value in the market place. Have them create campaigns to test. Have them on a retainer to keep you on track.

The biggest mistake businesses make is hiring a marketing agency for a one-off job, where the experts come in, focus the business, then are never hired back. The business goes right back to everything it was doing wrong and blames it on the marketing agency. Have the agency there frequently, for the life of the business.

Step 7

Hire a sales team that understand how to use the marketing elements you're putting to use. Give them not only great value ideas with irresistible offers, but commission incentives that will motivate them to create energy in the sales cycle. Your sales team and marketing agency or department should hold joint meetings on a regular basis (once a week). They should come up with offers that are show stoppers (WOW factors) and that they can aggressively push to get results within a 3-month time-frame. Align with the owners on the 3- month time frames to manage their expectations. Having time frames with real goals, builds calendars and punch lists that are success driven. Be aggressive and attentive to marketing systems daily, and you will be rewarded.

In the next book, we will explore how to train each person in the business to think in terms of your business' Mission Statements and 'Buyer Journey' specifically.

As you follow your buyer through the 12 stages of their journey to purchase your services/products, you will discover and experience the power of data in creating   bigger   business   growth.

Acknowledgements

Kyle McMurry

Neil Cohen

About Michel Gunn

I grew up in a modest household. I started working at the age of 11 because I liked making money. Having a compelling sales line got me many a babysitting gig.

After college, I moved to New York where I found my place in the Fashion Industry and had an illustrious career for about 12 years. I traveled many countries from East Asia, to India, Europe, the Caribbean Basin, and Canada, marketing and producing for big name labels such as Kenneth Cole and Sean John ('Puff Daddy'). The dichotomy of the different targets opened my eyes to so many aspects I could bring to small businesses.

As my first job, I was tasked with turning an almost purely production company into a leader in Boyswear, offering great design at a price. I had my ups and downs. I experimented with different unconventional marketing ideas, but, thank goodness, the owners saw I was headed somewhere even when certain turns returned nothing. The lessons were priceless. I learned value from listening to what the buyers wanted. I understood more and more what *the* audience wanted. By studying the targets, I became very good at dictating to the buyers what they needed to buy, because I could read the trends before they broke in addition to knowing how to translate them to their customers. Understanding how to create beauty that engaged a buyer to gravitate to my designs, was the key to everything. I studied human nature to understand behaviors, and from this understanding, I could then translate demand into supply for my employers.

I decided to leave the big-brand world to concentrate on growing small businesses in my home area. One of the things I was able to appreciate immediately is the lack of understanding of the buyer journey, among small business owners.

I knew immediately that I had found my calling and have dedicated myself since, to teaching small business owners how to be strategic thinkers. I translate customer behavior into actionable plans that are strategic and that yield sustainable growth.

I love to educate, and I'm happy to be doing it in New York, where I can see small businesses grow beyond their imagination. I believe that this will further humanity and I want to be part of that.

Next from Michel Gunn....

- Not your Grandfather's guide to Defining Your Small Business' Mission Statement and Buyer's Journey
- Not your Grandfather's guide to Sales Choreography
- Not your Grandfather's guide to inner office incentive programs

Before you go, please leave a review.

On Facebook: http://bit.ly/2Dqqiao

NOTES....